Life's Reflections

Life's Reflections

Thoughts and Poems

Charles Asbury

BOOKLOGIX
Alpharetta, Georgia

This book is fictitious. All references to ancient, historical events, persons living or dead, locations and places are used in a fictitious manner. Any other names, characters, incidents and places are derived from the author's own imagination. Similarities to persons living or dead, places, or events are entirely coincidental.

Copyright © 2013, 2023 by Charles Asbury
Second Edition 2023

All rights reserved. No part of this book may be reproduced or transmitted in any form or by any means, electronic or mechanical, including photocopying, recording, or any information storage and retrieval system, without permission in writing from the author.

ISBN: 978-1-6653-0639-3

This ISBN is the property of BookLogix for the express purpose of sales and distribution of this title. The content of this book is the property of the copyright holder only. BookLogix does not hold any ownership of the content of this book and is not liable in any way for the materials contained within. The views and opinions expressed in this book are the property of the Author/Copyright holder, and do not necessarily reflect those of BookLogix.

∞This paper meets the requirements of ANSI/NISO Z39.48-1992 (Permanence of Paper)

060923

I dedicate this book to the beautiful young women who captured my heart forever with the look of love in their eyes.

Looking For Love

Look to your right
Look to your left
Look with an open heart
Look all around you
Love is waiting to be found
Look again and again
Don't give up
Love will find you

The Soft Voice

I awake to a soft voice.
It calls me to arise from my slumber,
To go out into the world to observe the people.
To find love and give love.
To bring hope for a better future to everyone I meet.
To show strength in the face of danger.
To be truthful when others want you to lie.
To have compassion for those in need of help.
To show respect for the wonders of nature.
To be curious about people and their history.
To be a seeker of knowledge.
The day is done, time to rest.
Tomorrow and every day thereafter,
I will go out into the world to observe
And learn about the people of the world.

The Dark Glasses

I leave my room.
I walk through the streets.
I see the blue sky turn gray.
The buildings tower over me.
I feel so alone, my heart aches.
The people pass me in salience their love,
Hidden behind dark glasses.
I turn down a lonely street.
I go inside to my room.
I must rest, for tomorrow I will walk
among the people with the dark glasses again.
I will not give up.
I know love can be found among the
people with the dark glasses.

Beginnings

I look toward the stars
I feel the power of the universe
The place where all life began
The universe is ever-changing
This is the way it's been since
The beginning, and so it will remain

The Circle of Life

Our circle of life starts out very small and
As we grow, it gets bigger and bigger.
Then, as time goes by and we get older,
The circle becomes smaller and smaller again.
Then, one day, the circle of life is finished,
Leaving our spirit free to be reborn again
and begin the Circle of Life for someone else.

A Clearing in the Woods

I stand in silence and I'm inspired by
The snow-covered mountains towering over me.
All is quiet. I feel the wind on my face and the warmth of
the sun.
The sky is a brilliant blue with scattered thin white clouds.
I wonder, *Is this a dream I'm having or have I been
Transported to this place by some spirit or something?*
Then I feel the press of the people around me,
Rushing to work in the buildings that tower over me.
Oh, how I miss that magical moment and feeling
Of those mountains and the silence. Even if it was
Just a dream.

The Spirit Speaks

I listen for the spirit to give me the words to
Express my feelings about life.
I never know when the spirits will
Speak to me. I must be patient.
The words come to me in a flash, like a
Sudden summer thunderstorm.
Then the spirit is gone just as fast.

Valuable Things

In this world, there are many material things
People strive and hunger for
That are thought to be irreplaceable like
Gold and great sums of money.
To me, there are things far more valuable
than any amount of gold or money.
To me, the most valuable things in this world
are the spoken and written word of the people.
For every person in the world is truly one of a kind
and irreplaceable. Long live the words of the people.

The Sun

I stand in the sun and let its warmth flow over me
I feel its energy flow through every part of me
I'm renewed in body and spirit

Chocolate Cake

Be happy, take a break, and get yourself
A piece of chocolate cake and a
Glass of cold milk.

The Edge

I stand at the edge of the shore.
I feel the power of the sea drawing me
Into the deep blue water.
Then I feel the grasp of someone pulling me
From the depths of the deep blue waters.
I'm lying on the beach fighting for the
Breath of life to return to me.
I look around for my savior.
I'm alone, lying on the beach,
Feeling the warmth of the sun
And soft breezes caressing my body.
Sometimes, we are brought to the
Brink of destruction to be saved by
An unknown and unseen force.

The Wind's Voice

I hear and feel the forces of the planet
When the wind engulfs me.
I feel and smell the salty air from the
Depth of the deep blue sea,
The fragrance of the evergreens,
And the flowers of the deep woods.
The hot dry air of the great deserts.
The hot and humid air of the jungle.
The polluted air of the crowded and noisy cities.
The wind is the voice of the planet.

The Full Moon

The full moon hangs in the dark night sky, so close
It seems that one could touch it.
It glows like a bright silver ball covered
With millions of bright white lights.
It's a wondrous sight to see,
The air is clean and fresh,
The wind is calm with a bit of chill,
All of nature is quiet and resting,
Under the glow of the full moon.
It's a night to be in awe of nature
and to remember forever.

Cookies

I have a secret to tell you.
It's not of a dark deed from my past.
It's not of a long-lost love.
It's if you see me looking sad, here's all you need
To do to bring a smile to my face.
Just bring me a cookie, please.
Some say the chocolate chip is sublime,
That the sugar cookie is sweet and tangy.
I say the best of all is the sweet and soft oatmeal raisin.
Now you know my secret.
So, the next time you see me looking sad, I hope
You'll remember to bring me a cookie, please, to lift
My spirits and put a smile back on my face.

Joy for Today

Today is the day, not tomorrow,
To bring joy and peace into your life.
For no one knows what tomorrow will bring.
So, don't waste any time, start now.
People of faith tell us to wait for our days
Of peace and joy in the hereafter,
After our bodies have been
Laid to rest in the cold dark earth.
I say, why must we wait?
I say, why not fill our lives with joy
And peace now, before we are
Laid to rest in the cold dark earth?

Limitless

Every day of every living thing on this planet
is made up of the past, the present,
the future, combined into every second,
of every minute, of every hour
the planet continues to exist in
this limitless universe

Living 101

To be alive is to be
To be in love
To know joy
To know sadness
To be surprised
To be frightened
To be a friend
To win when no one thought you could
To help without expecting anything in return
To do all these things and more

The Forest

The leaves have fallen from the trees.
There's a chill in the fall air.
I long to walk through the forest.
The fallen leaves crunch under my feet.
I long to hear the sounds of the mighty waterfalls and streams.
To me, there's no place more beautiful or peaceful
Than the forest of this world—that's where I feel at home.

The Future

We all often think about the future
And what kind of life we'll have.
Some of us find our passion early in life
And pursue it with all their being.
Others just take life as it comes.
Either way, one must remember
That everything in life is subject to change,
And the two biggest forces of change
Are fate and love, which both
Are beyond our control.

The Road

Our life starts out like a new road.
The asphalt is black and shiny,
The markings are bright and easy to see,
The road is a pleasure to drive on,
Then as time goes by the road changes.
The asphalt is dull and the markings have
Faded, making them hard to follow.
We keep using the same road to
Get to our destination.
We do the same with our lives,
Staying on the bad roads, waiting for
Someone else to fix the road for us.

The First Day

It's 00:01:59 of the first day of the New Year.
It's time to forget the past.
It's time to make plans for a new you.
It's time to push forward with your dreams.
It's 00:02:59 on the first day of the New Year.
It's time to forget the past.
It's time to make plans for a new you.
It's time to push forward with your dreams.
So it goes, every second, of every minute, of every hour,
of every day, until 12:59:59 at the end of the year,
And then it starts all over again.
Such is the nature of time repeating
Itself again and again until there's
No more time for us.

The Joyful Mind

When you're stressed, stop. Take a deep breath,
Let it out slowly, close your eyes,
And let your mind help you relax.
For the mind is a wonderful thing. It holds all kinds
Of joyful memories that have just been waiting for
You to recall in times of stress, to bring us peace.

My Lover's Eyes

The grandeur of the Grand Canyon
Is a wondrous thing to see
So, too, are the forest and the
Majestic mountains of the world
The rain forest with its amazing plants and animals
All of these things are wondrous to see
But to me, the most beautiful sight to see
Is the look of love I see
When I look into my lover's eyes

A Beautiful Thing, Ice Cream

Attention, please! Attention, please!
There's a creation that's among the
Greatest the world has ever known.
It brings joy to everyone that
Comes in contact with it.
It's used by people of all ages and
Found in every part of the world.
Can you figure out what it is?
It's not a new phone or tablet or a big-screen TV.
It can be had in a single, a double, a triple.
It brings back the fun of being
A kid again if you're over twenty-one.
It's that delicious, wonderful,
Oh, so satisfying a thing!
Everyone loves ice cream!

The Blank Page

I look at the blank page with pen in hand ready to
Bring the thoughts about life lingering
Deep within my soul to the page.
I keep waiting for the spirits
To speak to me, but they are resting.
I believe that there are
Spirits that guide me in my quest
To express my thoughts about life.
I believe the same spirits are there for
All of us to help guide us in whatever we do.
For now, the spirits are silent, I will lay
The pen aside until their voices call me again to
Express my most deep feelings.

Power and Love

The history of humanity is
A long and complex one.
It's a history of many forces at work.
Two of these forces have not changed
Since the beginning of time.
It's the quest for power.
The other is the need to find love.
And, so it will remain until the
End of the world.

Love's Adventure

My love, come walk with me
Down a county lane, arm and arm.
My love, come with me and let
Me hold you gently in my arms
While we watch the sunset
From a beautiful tropical island.
My love, come with me and
I'll show you the bright lights of
Times Square and New York City.
We'll go shopping in Paris
and have dinner atop the Eiffel Tower.
My love, take my hand, my
Heart, let us begin our adventure
In love, forever.

Words

The words flow from my
Mind like the streams of the
Forest after a spring rain fast and deep.
Sometimes, like a stream after a summer
Drought, slow and shallow.
Sometimes, the words come to me
Straight and true without interruption.
Sometimes, the words come to me
In short bursts, day or night.
For when the words will come to me again,
I cannot say, only the spirits know.

The Art of Relaxation

There's a place I go when
The worries of the world get to be
Too much, and you can too.
You don't need to take a long drive in your car
Or buy a plane ticket to some far-off place.
All you need to do is just follow these simple steps.
First, find a quiet spot.
Second, close your eyes,
Take a deep breath, and let it out slowly.
Third, imagine yourself in the
Most beautiful place you've ever been,
And let your inner spirit do the rest.
So, the next time the pressures of the
Living get to be too much, just remember:
One . . . two . . . three . . .

Peace and Anxiety

To live in a world of peace or
Anxiety is a choice
We make every day of our lives.
It's a choice only we can make,
Even though the job of living in
Today's world may seem
To make it impossible to have a choice,
We have the power to
Overcome whatever keeps
Us from finding peace and joy.
We just have to bring forth the power
Of our inner spirit, and desire.
So, I say again it's your choice to
Live in a world filled with peace or anxiety.

Beautiful Roses

The once-beautiful roses sit in a tall crystal vase,
Waiting for someone to replace them.
Their once-bright red silky petals are dry and faded.
Their once-bright green leaves are dark and brittle.
It's the same with so many things in our lives
That have lost their beauty and usefulness or so it seems.
But to the owner of the dry and faded roses,
She sees them as they once were,
fragrant and soft to the touch.
They remind her of the first time
she held her lover in her arms
As they danced through the night.

The New World

There's another world that I've seen.
It's a world where the skies are a vibrant
Blue with patches of big white clouds.
The trees and the plants cover the land
Like a patchwork quilt with its beautiful colors.
The ocean is pristine, teaming with fish of all sizes.
The fresh sparkling waters of the lakes and streams,
Like the oceans, are teaming with life.
The air is pure and fresh, filled with the
Sweet melodies of songbirds.
The only ambition of the people of this
World is to bring peace and joy to one another.
You say this is only a foolish dream of my imagination.
I say maybe you're right, but what if the people
Were to stop fighting for power over one another and make
It the law of the nations to bring peace and joy to each other?
Think what it would be like, just take a moment and
Think about it, that's all I'm asking.

Worry No More

You can worry about tomorrow
From sunrise until sunset, or
You can take action to make your day better.
For tomorrow will come as it has
For millions and millions of years,
And millions of more to come, give or
Take a couple million,
So, at the end of the day, close your eyes
And rest your mind and body.
Get a good night's sleep
And, decide to have a better day tomorrow.

The Color Yellow

The color yellow is a bright and happy color
It brings a smile to my face
When I see a field of sunflowers or daffodils
Or a bunch of yellow roses on my kitchen
Table with the morning sun shining on them
Or a bright yellow convertible
With a beautiful woman with her long blond
Hair blowing in the wind as she passes me on the freeway
Or a bunch of young kids playing on the beach
With a bright-yellow beach ball
Ah, yes, the color yellow sure does bring
A smile to this old man's face

The Changing Winds

The wind blows through the trees
Sending the yellow and red leaves of
Autumn surging through the air
Sparkling like jewels in the sun.
The wind blows over the desert sands,
Shifting the fine grains of sand from
One dune to another, over and over again.
The wind blows and the seas rise
And fall all around the planet.
The mighty wind is forever moving
And changing the planet.

Spring

Spring is in the air
The sun is warm and
Nature's bright colors can
Be seen everywhere
The sounds of *"let's play ball"*
And *"get your hot dog"*
And *"ice-cold drinks right here"*
Can be heard in small towns
And large cities
Lovers young and old
Walk along the shore and
Down a county lane
Arm and arm

Heat Wave

The sun is blazing hot
The air is hot and dry
Suddenly dark clouds appear
Bringing heavy rains to cool the earth
Just as the earth gets over-heated from
The sun and needs cooling down
We get overheated and need the
Cooling rain of a thunderstorm
So that we can continue on with our lives

The Sidewalk

The sidewalk was once smooth and level,
But now it is cracked and broken
With weeds growing between the cracks.
All is not lost with a little work,
The sidewalk can be made new again,
The cracks patched, the
Broken pieces replaced and the weeds pulled up.
The same can be done to our lives,
When we become broken and the weeds try to take over.
All it takes is the desire to change,
And the love of others who have been
Through the same hard times as you
To bring you back to a world
Of purpose and joy.

The Place I Love

I've seen the cities of the world like:
New York
London
Berlin
Madrid
Bangkok
I've seen the mountains of America
South America and Europe
I've seen the volcanoes of South America
I've seen the Atlantic and Pacific oceans
It has been great to have seen all
These places, but there is nothing
That compares to the feeling
I get from the look and the touch
Of my love and my family
When the day is done

When the Leaves Fall

When the leaves have fallen from the trees,
You can see many things that were once hidden.
There's an old stone barn with
The bright rays of the sun streaming
Through the holes in the roof.
There's a small abandoned farmhouse
Where the laughter of small children
Could once be heard while their mother
Worked in the kitchen preparing supper for the family.
The children stand by the kitchen screen door waiting for
Their father to return from a hard day's work in the fields.
An old rusting tractor sits under a large oak tree
With weeds growing all around it.
These are some of the things you can see
When the leaves have fallen.

Colorful Clouds

Look to the skies and you will
See one of nature's greatest displays of color
There's the bright-blue skies of summer
With granitic white clouds
There's the dark gray and black clouds
Of a sudden thunderstorm
There's the beautiful orange, red,
purple and blues at sunset

Joyful Things

The touch of my lover's hand in mine
The laughter of a baby in my arms
The purring of a kitten sitting in my lap
Watching a young puppy running and jumping
Watching a woodpecker building his nest
The feeling of the sand between my toes
As I walk along the beach
Sitting in my overstuffed easy chair
Listening to my favorite Frank Sanatra tunes
This is my short list, what's yours?

Monday

You ask me what day it is?
I reply, Monday.
The next day you ask me,
What day it is?
I reply, Monday.
You say I'm wrong, today is Tuesday.
I reply that for me, I don't care about the
Date on the calendar.
For me, every day is Monday, and a chance
For a new beginning for a new journey
To face new challenges,
So, whenever someone asks me what
day it is, my reply is Monday.

The Forgotten America

I went for a drive to see the other America,
Out past the tall buildings and noise of the city.
I saw the rolling hills and small family farms.
I saw the small towns with a single
Traffic light with a combination convenience store,
Gas station, and a small family-owned dinner.
I saw abandoned houses with broken windows
And boarded-up businesses in small towns.
I saw a house in need of repair with an old,
Broken down car along with children's toys
And a trampoline in the front yard.
I saw an old man sitting on the front
Porches waving to me as I drove by.
This is the America most people
Don't see or think about.
This is the forgotten America.

The Old Man in the Train Station

A young man stands on the platform
With a bouquet of red roses,
Impatiently waiting for the train
To get home to his young bride.
A middle-aged man with a laptop bag
Slung over his shoulder is having
A very angry conversation with
Someone on his cell phone,
Impatiently walking back and forth,
He has to get home to finish the work
He didn't finish at the office.
An old man sits on a bench watching these men.
They remind him of what life was once like for him.
That was long ago now the old man has nowhere to go.
No deadlines to meet, no million-dollar
Deals to finish by the end of the month.
Now, it's just another day of people-watching
For the old man in the train station.

Friday

Today is payday
Today is the end of the work week for someone
Today is the beginning of the work week for someone
Today is someone's birthday
Today is someone's wedding day
Today is someone's retirement party
Today someone will graduate college
Today someone will buy their first car
Today someone will buy their first house
Today is Friday
Go find someone to love
Today is Friday
Be happy

Say I Love You

There are many ways to say I Love You
You can write a beautiful love song
You can write a beautiful romantic poem
You can go on a romantic cruise around the world
You can do all of these things
But what the love of your life
Will always remember is just take her in your arms
And say these three simple words: I LOVE YOU

Opportunity

What is the one word that describes what we all want?
No, it's not the words that one usually thinks
Of like wealth, fame, power, or love.
You see, in order to get any of those things,
First, you need to have the opportunity to show someone
That you're the best leader, idea person, manager,
Or that you will love someone with all
Your heart and soul for the rest of your life.
I say again the word is "opportunity," for without it
Nothing can happen to change your life for the better.
It doesn't matter what a person's econometrics,
social states, or nationally may be.
Now go find your opportunity or make one happen.

Doubt

There's one word that stops individuals
From finding the love of their life
Or turning their dreams into reality.
That word is doubt, and it has
No regard for gender or education.
Take heart, for everyone that's been
Successful has had to deal with their own
Doubts about the future, but they
Overcame them and pressed on.
So, press on with your dreams.

Questions About Life

I sit and think about my future.
Will I be healthy?
Will I have financial success?
Will I have love in my life?
Then a feeling of urgency comes
Over me to stop all this thinking about
The future, to get up and turn the hourglass
Over and face the challenges of
The future, as a wise man once told me,
It's ever too late to change,
So I better be getting to it.

Feeling Good

When the sun shines and the skies
are a bright blue I feel happy.
When the sky's dark with storm clouds I feel sad.
I see a couple of young lovers holding hands, I feel happy.
I watch the waves crash on the shore and I
Want to go sailing on the ocean blue,
To see what's over the horizon.
I see someone helping a stranger in trouble and I feel hope
For the future of mankind.
I feel a cold breeze, it chills my body through and through.
I feel the warmth of the sun and my body
Feels warm through and through.
The stars shine brightly in the night sky and
I close my eyes and sleep in peace.

'57 T-Bird

It's a wonderful life
The sun's a shining
I'm riding down the highway
In my bright red '57 T-bird
With my sweetheart beside me
Listening to Ray Charles sing
"Georgia on My Mind"
Like I say, life's a wonderful thing

Those Loving Eyes

I hear a sweet tender love song
and I'm filled with joyful memories
I'm transported back to the first time
I saw the look of love in my lover's eyes
Ah it's so sweet that look of love in
My lover's eyes, a look that stays
Fresh in my mind, never changing
A look that keeps me forever young
That wonderful look and feeling of love

The Human Voice

The sound of the human voice can be
A beautiful thing when words of love
Are heard

The End of Work

Today is the end of another workweek
In our cubical, be it big or small
We all look forward to the day
When we can stop working in
Our cubicles and be free to pass
The time as we please enjoying
The rest of our days
Some say this isn't so
They live to work, but I think
Secretly they, too, look forward
To the day when they can
Leave their cubical and do
Just do as they please

Peaceful Skies

The sky is filled with row after
Row of great bellowing white clouds
Taller and grander than any mountain
On earth moving softly and peacefully
Across the bright blue sky
They bring joy and comfort to
My soul and spirit helping to
Remind me of the power
Of the creator

The Storm

The summer day starts out with bright
Blue skies with soft scatted white
Clouds and a cool breeze rushing
Through the leaves of the trees.
Then, without warning, the bright
Blue skies are filled with dark gray
And black storm clouds block out
The sun turning day into night.
Thunder rumbles and rolls
And shakes the sky.
Rain and hail fall from the sky,
Filling the streets and streams.
Lightning flashes light up the dark
Sky and strike the ground with such
Force that it shakes, trees split apart
And houses are torn apart.
Then, just as quickly, the storm clouds
Roll away. The thunder, the rain, the hail
And the lightning all stop.
The bright blue summer sky returns
And a cool breeze rushes through the
Leaves of the trees again.

Passion

There's a word that is often
Used when one tries to convey their
Depth of emotion when speaking
Of love and hate, the word passion
The word passion should be used
To convey the emotions of love not hate
The world would be so much
Better off with more love than hate

Time

Time is something we all take for
Granted until we need more of it.
But it doesn't work that way, no
Matter how we wish it would.
So, keep this thought with you
And remember to watch what you
Say or do, because once you've
Used the time you have, for whatever reason,
It's gone and there's no turning
Back the hands of time.

Wandering Thoughts

I often ask people this simple question,
Where do their thoughts wander off to?
Do their thoughts take them back to a
Walk along the seashore on a bight
Summer day with their sweetheart?
Do their thoughts have them standing
On the summit of a snow-capped
Mountain looking at the
World beneath their feet?
Do their thoughts take them to
Far-off places filled with smiling
Faces and beautiful sights to see?
Do their thoughts have them sailing
Upon the oceans of the world
In search of their island paradise?
The power of the mind can cause
Our thoughts to wander off to all kinds
Of places like these and many more.
I say turn your wandering thoughts into reality
And and begin your wandering.

Time Control

Scientists have been able to split the atom
And harness its power, but there's
One thing that no one has ever
Been able to control—that's time.
Only in the movie or in a
Science-fiction novel has man been
Able to make time stand still,
Go backward or forward.
A truer statement has never
Been said; that time stands still for no one.
So, it has always been and so it will remain,
Until everything falls into the black hole of space.

Remembrances

I sit under a shaded tree on
A bright summer day and let
The worries of the day fade away.
I let my thoughts wander where
They will and I remember the
Raspy voice of Louis Armstrong singing
"Hello Dolly," Ray Charles's soulful
"Georgia On My Mind," Willie Nelson's
Rendition of "On The Sunny Side Of The Street."
My spirits are lifted and a smile comes to my face.
All is right with the world.

Good Health

If you want to enjoy good
Health, take a break go outside and
Find a shaded tree or a park bench.
Take a seat and clear your mind of all you
Have to do today and tomorrow.
Just focus on the sounds of
Nature all around you and
In a very short time you will
Be a more peaceful and happier person.

Decisions and People

We all make decisions about people too often, too soon.
Such was the case in a story I read about two people,
A young man thought to be
Irresponsible by a fellow coworker
But that feeling was turned into one
Of respect and gratitude when
She saw how he went about taking
Care of the people that others had no time for.
Then that respect and gratitude turned
Into an opportunity for the
Young man to spread joy and
Kindness to more people.
This story shows what can happen
When a person is open to a change of heart
And that we all should learn not to
Be so quick to judge another person.

Small Children

There's something unique about small children
That I've noticed no matter where I go
It seems that small children think
That they should be the center of attention
And, quite frankly I for one agree

Power of Music

Music is a window into the
Soul and spirit of the individual
For us to see the true thoughts and
Emotions about the things at happen
In their lives from falling in love
To losing someone dear to them, or
Missing the chance to make their
Dreams come true

The Stroke

The day begins as every other day.
We go about the business of living,
Making our way through the day and
Back home again safely, then we feel
A crushing pain in our chest and it's hard to
Breathe and we think that the end is near.
We fight against the fear, hopeful
That we will have another day
And a second chance to make a
Better life for ourselves and the
Ones we hold dear in our heart.
So remember to say I Love You
To those you hold dear in your heart
Before you go out the door.

My Writer's Nook

The room is quiet
I'm alone with my thoughts
And I can't seem to stop
Writing them down one
After another, then
The spell is broken
The room is filled
With the sounds
And thoughts of others
The urgency of
Writing down my
Thoughts is gone
Until the room is
Quiet again

Problems

Problems are a normal part of life,
The question is how do we solve them?
First, we need to find out what's
Causing the problem?
Second, we need to find the best
Way to solve the problem.
Then finally we need to put
The solution into action,
Giving it all our energy and faith.

The Beauty of Humanity

Humanity is made up of people of
All different shapes, sizes, and colors.
We all have a heart, lungs, a brain and
Many other things that keep us alive,
But there are a couple of things that
Are unique to every person that can not
Be duplicated or replaced because they
Are not of a physical nature.
The things I'm writing about are the soul
And a person's thoughts.

The Young Woman

I see the young couple dancing.
Their bodies becoming one, swaying
And spinning around and around on the dance floor
To the beat of the music and its passion.
Ah, to be in the arms of a beautiful woman
And feeling all the passion of the dance.

Our Changing Emotions

Sometimes the sunny skies turn dark and
The wind blows hard and the rain comes down hard.
Then the sunny skies return and the
Blustery winds and the hard rains disappear.
Such is the way of nature and our human emotions.

The Refrigerator Door

You can find out what's really important
To a family by just looking at
The things on the refrigerator door.
You'll see things like drawings by the
Kids of Mom, Dad, Brother, Sister
And the family dog or cat.
You'll see Mom's to-do list
With the kids' schedules for
Sports or dance lessons.
You'll find the refrigerator door
Magnetic from the family vacation

What you're really seeing on the refrigerator door
Are the signs of a family sharing their love.

Percussion

The world has changed in many ways and it has
Been said by many scholars that mankind has come
A long way in promoting equality and justice for all,
But the percussion of people because of their
Religious beliefs, ethnic origins, and physical appearance
Is still at work in much of the world of the twenty-first century.
Will it ever stop? I fear not until mankind is brought to
The edge of total destruction, hopefully I am wrong.

Bands of Gold

We place bands of gold on our fingers to show the
World that we are one, and off we go to face the
Challenges of the world together, joyful and
Confident that over time the commitment and love
That we share with each other that led
Us to place those bands of gold upon our fingers
Will not wavier and disappear, for the bands of
Gold are not important—the important thing is
The commitment and love we professed that day
Before the world for each other, that's the thing that will
Keep those bands of gold upon our fingers
Until the end of time

Emotions

It is something very unique about the human
Need to feel the emotions of love and joy
In their own life and through the lives of others
Like when we see a couple in a loving embrace or when we
Watch children laughing and playing in the park with
Their parents—those are the physical displays of love
That everyone can understand
But why do we even feel the same emotions of
Love and happiness when we know that it's just a story
From someone's imagination? Just take a moment
And think about how many times you've heard
Someone say how a movie, play, book, or poem
Brought them to tears . . . that it all seemed so real
Stop and think for a moment that without the
Ability to feel emotions like love and happiness we
Wouldn't be human would we—so let us be glad
For the ability to feel emotions like love and joy

The Wealthy Man

I once knew a man that was very wealthy
And he often said that when he had enough
Money, he was going to fulfill his lifelong dream
Of taking his money and spending the rest of his days
On the beach of an island paradise in the Pacific.
He never did stop and spend time on that island in
The Pacific—instead he just kept waiting until he had
Just a little more money . . . then it was too late.
I write this sad tale as a warning to others so they
Won't be like my friend and wait until
It's too late to live their lifelong dream.

The Light

There's an old saying that there's always
A light at the end of the tunnel but when
Someone is trying to resolve their
Problems, that light seems
A long, long way off. Don't give up
The creator will show you the light.

The Imperfect Universe

The people of the world are always
Searching for the latest displays of
Outward perfection for everyone to copy
But people seem to forget that there is nothing
Perfect in this world or in the universe

Refreshing the Mind

The older we get the more we need
To keep our minds in tip-top shape
So we need to take time to learn
About all the new things and stuff
Going on in this ever-changing world

Our Importance

Sometimes we feel that we are the most
Important person in the group, that we are the
Boss's right-hand man, as the old saying goes,
Then, one day we are replaced without really
Knowing why. So remember this one very
Important fact of life: change is the
One thing that you can count on no matter
Your position in this world.

The Final Frontier

Space, the final frontier.
But how can that be?
If something is final,
That means there
Isn't any more of it or
That there's a stopping point.
So that means
There aren't any more
Planets, moons, stars
Galleries, meteors
For us to find and learn about.
I think there is always something new to
Discover, so the phrase should
Be changed to:
Space the ongoing challenge.

The Bonnie Lass

There once was a beautiful woman
From the land of leprechauns and shamrocks.
Her soft fiery red hair
Falling in beautiful curls across
Her shoulder and down her back.
Her eyes were as green as the
Heath on the moors.
Her smile was as bright and
Warm as the morning sun
Rising from the sea.
And when I hear the song "Danny Boy,"
Oh! how it brings a little
Tear to my eyes for the
Land of my ancestors.
Someday, I will come again to see the
Green hills of Ireland
But until then, the memory of the beautiful woman
With the fire-red hair, green eyes,
And her sweet voice singing
"Danny Boy" will keep the land
Of my ancestors in my heart.

The View

We speed through life trying to beat
The stoplights, never slowing down
To enjoy the view along the way

The Glorious Rain

The rain replenishes the rivers, lakes, and streams
It brings much-needed moisture to the soil and plants
Which in turn replenishes our lives

The Color Red

When I think of the color red
I think of ripe red strawberries
I think of ripe red raspberries
I think of ripe red cherries
I think of red velvet cake
I think of fast red sports cars
I think of red skies at sunset
I think of dozens of red roses
I think of beautiful women in red dresses
I think of red heart-shaped boxes of
Valentine's Day chocolates

Music

Music is one of the greatest creations of humanity
It brings joy to everyone young and old
It gives everyone a way to express their feelings
It brings healing to the soul in times of trouble

Embrace

Every day we should take time to remember the look of love
In our lover's eyes and their warm embrace comforting us

Respect

Sometimes we forget that we are
One of nature's greatest creations
And forget to treat ourselves and others
With the respect we all deserve

Humility

Humility is something that's seems
To be in short supply in this world

My Life History

I was twenty-one with no plan for the future, just having fun.
Then I was thirty with the love of my life,
A son, a daughter, a great career.
Then I was forty and all was well with my
Family and my career.
Then I was fifty and life was changing, our son was
In medical school, our daughter was a journalist.
Then I was sixty, at the top of my profession
And the house was filled with the sounds of grandchildren.
Then I was seventy, taking it easy, writing my thoughts about
Life while my wife was planning our trip around the world.
Now I'm eighty and enjoying the memories of all the
Good times I've had and taking life one day at a time.

Power of Laughter

To improve your health find something to have
A good laugh about at least once a day

Good Days, Bad Days

Our life is filled with both good and bad days, hopefully we'll have more good days to remember than bad

Summertime

It's finally summertime
Time to fill the long hot summer days
And nights with the stored-up passion
Of those cold gray days of winter
It's time for June brides
It's time for walks on the beach
It's time for family barbacues
It's time for little league baseball games
It's time to have fun in the sun
It's time to make memories for the cold gray
Days of winter when they come again

Detours

As long as you know where you're
Going don't worry about the detours
You may face along the way

GPS

Just think, with a smartphone
And a GPS app you
Might never need to ask anyone
For directions again

The Novel

Take time and write that great novel
You've been putting off forever and
See how your life changes

My Protector

My friend, my protector, why have you forsaken me?
You have been with me through all the good and bad times.
No one else knows my inner thoughts and all my fears.
Don't leave me in this cruel world alone and defenseless.
Oh, how the mind plays tricks on us when it becomes
Filled with doubt and we lose trust in the power of the
Spirit that the creator has created within us
To be our lifelong friend and protector.

The Shade Tree

I never saw a shade tree that
I didn't enjoy being around
Unfortunately, I can't say the same
Thing about some of the people I've met

Our Days

The days of our lives are sometimes filled with things
That we do over and over, like caring for the people we love

Why? Why?

I raise my head toward the heavens.
I ask the creator to look down on this world.
I ask that the poverty and hardship of the
People be taken away.
I ask that peace and compassion be
Brought to all the peoples of the world.
I get no reply to my cries of anger and
despair that come from the depths of my soul.
I go to the scholars of the world and
Ask them why the creator doesn't answer me?
They say that I must be patient, that the
Creator sees the troubles in the world,
That the creator will do all that I ask when the time is right.
I'm like a small child, I cannot wait.
I want the creator to do as I ask, now.
I don't know what to do, should
I keep crying out to the creator?
Or am I to be patient like the scholars say?
I study on the matter and see that all
I can do is wait and hope for a better tomorrow
And help those around me to have
A better life today.

Lovers on the Beach

My love will come sit with me and
Watch the young lovers on the beach
And we'll remember when we were
Young lovers too

Hallelujah

Good morning world, I'm so glad
The creator has granted me
Another day to enjoy
The sights and sounds of the world
HALLELUJAH

Bowl of Grits

Life is a lot like a bowl of grits.
They're real easy to make,
But if you don't watch what you're doing,
It's real easy to mess up.
Which isn't a problem with grits,
You just throw them away and try again,
But in life, if you mess up something the first time around,
You might not get another chance to do it over again.
So pay attention to what you're doing
And do it right the first time.

Good Night's Sleep

If you want a good night's sleep
Exercise your body and fill your
Mind with peaceful thoughts
And nature will do the rest

Unfinished Business

Sometimes I think that I'm the only one with
Unfinished dreams and desires
Then I see the look on other peoples faces'
When they think of dreams and desires lost
Then I know having these unfinished dreams and desires
Of mine are just part of being human

The Old House

There's an old house in a small village
High in the Andes Mountains of Ecuador.
It stands empty and quiet.
Some of the tiles are missing from the roof,
The plaster walls are cracked,
And the wooden floors are covered with dust.
In the living room, there's an old faded photo
Of a young couple hanging on the wall.
As I walk through the house, I feel the spirit
Of the couple in the photograph and their love
For each other and their family.
It surrounds me and I feel a sense of peace.
In one of the bedrooms I find an old trunk
Filled with children's books and love letters
From a young man to his future wife
And a small leather-bound family Bible.
May the spirit of love I found in the old house
Stay with me forever.

Success

I say to myself sometimes,
Boy, it sure would be nice if
One of my big ideas came true,
Then I could buy that bright
Red convertible for me and my honey,
And we could go cruising
Down the boulevard in style.
Then she gives a hug and a kiss
And I don't need that big red convertible.

My Friend Sallie

I once had a friend named Sallie
She wasn't much of a talker
She didn't care what kind of car I drove
Or how much money I had
She was always there for me
When I was feeling down and in the dumps
She knew just how to cheer me up
My friend is gone but never forgotten
I was feeling alone and depressed
So I decided to go for a ride
And there I was, at the place where
I had seen Sallie for the first time
I didn't want to go in but I knew
That she would want me to
So into the animal shelter, I went
And there I found Susie, with
Her big bright brown eyes and
A loving gentle disposition
So, I took Susie home with me, and now
Both of our lives are filled with joy

Thunder

The thunder's so loud that
People cry out in pain.
The lighting strikes the earth and it shakes
And the forests are turned into raging infernos.
The rain comes down, filling the
Rivers and streams, causing them
To overflow and carry everything away
In their path to the sea.
The dark clouds cover the sky until the
Rays of the sun are gone,
And everyone feels that the end must be near.
Someone cries out, "Please spare this world and its people!"
The turmoil stops and the world and its people
Are spared this time by the creator of all things.

Fortune Cookie

When you get a fortune cookie
You never know what your fortune will be
Until you break the cookie apart and read
What's on the little slip of paper inside
So it is with our life
We never know what awaits us
Until we awake from our night's sleep
And walk out our front door
To start our day

Confusion

There's a new human condition that I've come across
It's called the Human Mental Confusion Condition
And there's no cure for it
It's when we live life in harmony with ourselves and others
Then other times we live our life like others think we should
It's confusing, I know, but that is just the way life is sometimes

Empty Space

It's nothing. It's emptiness.
Still, we all want our own personal space.
A place where we can say and think whatever we want.
A place to take a break from the insanity of the world.
There's a place where we can
Experience this that's often overlooked.
It's the vast expanse of our own mind.
I call it the Enter Mind Experience.

Free Spirit

Sitting in the park on a cool summer's night
Listening to some Beatles tunes
The people are clapping and singing along
Children, couples, young and old are dancing
A father dances with his young children
The vibes from the music fill my heart with joy
And brings me back to an easier
Time in my life and I'm a free spirit
Again for a few wonderful moments

Face of Love

A young child stands alone in a group of people,
In the park with a look of joy and love on their face.
The people are left speechless for a few moments,
Then they too start to feel the love coming from the
Soul of the child and they too have a look
Of joy and love on their faces.
This is the power of the pure love of a child.

The Oak Tree

The majestic oak tree stands alone on a little noel,
In the middle of a field of tall grass like a
Knight standing guard over his master's property.
The tree's huge branches, thick with green leaves,
Provides shade for those that come to visit the small
Cemetery of the people that first settled in this land.
Soon, the green leaves of summer will turn
Yellow, red, and wither away with the coming of
Winter, leaving the branches bare
Where the battle scars of its many
Clashes with nature can be seen,
But the mighty tree holds on against the wind,
The lighting, the rain, and the wrath of nature.
Hopefully, man will let nature and the tree decide
When the battle between the two of them will end.

Wisdom

Wisdom is something one acquires over time
And something to be shared, but a person needs to know
When, where, and how best to share their wisdom
So that it's not wasted, but for the benefit of everyone.

The Hopeful Heart

Keep hope for a brighter future in your heart
For those days when life isn't going your way

The Greatest Achievement

Words are the greatest achievement of mankind.
Without words, there would be no way to create a language
For people to express their wants and needs to each other.
It's the twenty-first century,
the age of great scientific advances,
But the peace of the world still relies on the
Spoken and written word.
Hopefully the words of peace will be the
Words that the leaders
Of the world want to hear.

Until the End

The end of what?
The end of everything,
Including our own life.
No one knows when.
So, I'll just keep
Doing what I've always done.
I'll just keep putting one
Foot in front of another
And writing my thoughts
Down for whoever wants
To read them one at a time.
Until the end.

Another Day

Today is another day in our life
To feel the emotions of love
Joy sadness anger pain
One or more times during
The day before its time to
Let the darkest of nights engulf us
So that we can rest our mind
So that we can face another
Day in the world

The Rambling Rose

The rambling rose is a great rose
It rambles wherever it wants
Bringing its beautiful roses for everyone to see
It rambles along climbing the barbed wire fences
Up the side of the buildings and houses
It goes wherever the bees take its pollen
To all parts of the country
East, West, North, and South
Sometimes I wish I could be a rambling rose

My Machine

I sit in my machine, feeling safe in my own world.
Going from destination A to destination B
Like I do every day of my life,
Like all the other people in their machines around me.
The radio tuned to a station playing
The music from the '60s, '70s, '80s, and TODAY.
I ride along not thinking about anything,
Not about my problems or the problems of the world.
Just watching the bright blue sky
And the big white clouds roll by.
Sometimes, I wish that I could just keep
Going and going, safe and secure in my
Machine in my own world.
Then I'm brought back to reality,
When the traffic light turns green,
And my cell phone rings.

Cold Days

The hot days of summer are gone
The cool days of fall are here
The leaves on the trees are changing
From bright green to red and yellow
It's a beautiful time of year
So beautiful that you want to
Keep the sights and sounds of these
Beautiful fall days tucked away in your
Memory for those gray and cold winter days

Something to Say

Some will say that
There's nothing to write about
That hasn't already been written about
I say they are wrong
For as long as there's life on earth
There will always be stories to be written

Love

You love me
I love life
You love life
Everyone loves life
Today is good

Thoughts

my thoughts
some say are
sometimes
dumb
bright
wrong
interesting
uninteresting
funny
happy
sad
unique
etc. . . . etc. . . .

Pieces

What kind of poetry
Will I write today?
Will they be like the fragrant
And beautiful flowers of springtime
That bring joy and peace to our spirits?
Will they be like the fruits
And vegetables that give us
Strength and energy?
Or will I let my mind
Remain empty of any new thoughts
And let it wither away like fruit
On the vine in the hot, dry, summer sun?

Fire

I sit and watch the flames of the fire
Dance and jump in the night sky as the
Stump of an old pine tree burns.
I am captivated by the bright-red and orange flames
And the glow of the bright-red embers,
Much like the first human that
discovered fire must have been.
For with this one simple discovery, the human race
Stepped out of the darkness
And began the creation of the world we know now,
But no matter how advanced we become,
There's still something about
The bright-red and orange flames and the
Glowing red embers of fire that still captivate us.

Accomplishments

Enjoy your accomplishments and victories, my friend.
The small ones and the big ones.
Just remember you didn't get to where you are
All by yourself, that you had help along the way.
So be thankful for the help and kindness
You got from all the people you met along the way,
And remember to give someone else a helping hand
So they too can be victorious in life.

Day and Night

As day turns to night
The bright blue sky becomes dark.
The bright leaves of the trees become dull.
The warm and colorful flowers become dull.
And sometimes the same things happen in our life.
We let our world become dark and dull.
But we must do like nature and
Let the bright light of the sun
Bring the colors of the rainbow
Into our life each
And every day.

Seeing the World

I wonder what it would be like
To travel anywhere I wanted.
I wonder what it would be like
To sit on the beach and watch
The sunset over the Indian Ocean.
I wonder what it would be like
To sit and have a glass of wine
On a bright summer's day,
In a cafe in France or Spain.
Then someone asks for a copy
Of a report about something
And I'm brought back to reality.
The clock strikes 5:00 p.m.
And its time to go home,
To my love and I no longer
Think about a glass of wine in
France or Spain. All I'll ever need
waits for me at my front door.

Ancestors

My ancestors are with me
I hear my father's voice in mine
I see my mother's eyes when I look in the mirror
Sometimes they remind me of good times
Sometimes of sad times
I wonder when I'm gone
If any of those that I've left behind
Will want to hear my voice when
My spirit comes to visit them in the beyond
If they do I hope it will remind them of
The good times we shared

A Better Day

There's an old saying
A better day a coming
Sometimes it seems like
A better day a coming for sure
Then sometimes it seems
Like there's no way
All I can do until
That better day comes
Is keep my head up and
Do the best I can
And let the spirits
Of love and peace
Watch over me
Until that better day comes

The Quiet Stream

I remember one
Bright spring day
Sitting beside
A quiet stream,
Enjoying doing nothing.
Ah, that was so long ago.
Oh! How I wish
I could be that young boy again,
Sitting beside that quiet stream,
Enjoying having nothing to do,
Away from the trials of this life.

The Covered Soul

Like the piles of autumn leaves
That cover the ground
So too are the true feelings
And emotions of our soul
Covered for fear
Of what might happen if
They were uncovered for all to see

The World Wrapped in Love

Let the peoples' voices rise in praise
Let the trumpets make a joyful noise
Let the laughter of children be heard everywhere
Let the wind fill the air with the sweet fragrances of spring
Let the bright blue skies shine
Let the whole world be wrapped in LOVE
HALLELUJAH
Let me say it again
HALLELUJAH
To life, love, peace
For all of the world
Not just for a day
For eternity

The Sword of Humanity

The spirit of humanity can be
Like the double-edged sword
With one edge being love and peace
The other edge being hate and death

Anticipation

We all live in anticipation
Of finding the perfect love
Of finding the perfect career
Of finding the perfect home
Of creating the perfect family
Of living the perfect life
You say
NO! NOT ME!
Then you are one of the few and
I wish you a long and joyful life
Free of anticipation

Seeds of Peace

The seeds of peace are within all of us.
Sometimes they are cared
For in fertile soil with loving hands.
Sometimes they fall
Upon poor untended soil, but
One only needs to ask the creator
And his loving hands will
Give the care needed
For the seeds of
Peace within us to bloom
For all to see.

Lemons

There's an old saying
When life gives you lemons
Turn them into lemonade
I say add some things
Like love, hope, and faith
And make a smoothie that
Will make your life better
Not just for today
But for the rest of your life

Stay in the Light

There's a dark side to the world
Be careful it can overpower you
It can make you feel lost and alone
Your dreams and hopes
For a better future
Seem lost too
All those that
Once stood by you
Seem to have gone away
Then you see a ray of light
Shining through the darkness
Walk toward the light
And with each step you take
Your dreams and hopes for a
Better future grows stronger and stronger

Peace Be with You

I say to you,
Peace be with you.
You hear but you don't listen.
You turn away.
I say to the people,
Peace be with you.
The people hear,
But they too don't listen, they too turn away.
But I will keep saying to everyone I meet,
Peace be with you.
For as long as one person keeps saying the words,
Peace be with you,
There's hope that somehow someday,
The words will come true.

Suspended in Time

I stand looking at the sky filled with billowing
Clouds taller than any building on earth.
There's silence all around me.
For a few seconds,
I'm alone in the world,
Seemly suspend in time
Even though the
Things of the physical
World surround me.
My mind is filled with
So many thoughts,
The only words I can find
To express my feelings are
Being one with the universe.
Oh, such a feeling is almost
Indescribable.

Master of Verse and Rhyme

Master of the verse and rhyme,
Come give us a poem about
Love, hope, courage,
The stars, the universe, the human soul,
The passion of a woman's love,
So that we may learn
How to have a better life,
There and now.
My friends, I say to you
Look to yourself and the
Power of the creator
For what you seek.

Cathedrals in the Sky

Clouds are a wondrous thing.
Sometimes, they are thin and long, like
Pieces of cotton candy.
Sometimes, they are immense bright-white formations,
One piled on top of another,
Grander than any mountain on earth.
Sometimes, they are massive dark things hovering
So close to the earth, that one's afraid they will fall to
Earth and smash everything into pieces.
When the sun goes down, they light up the evening sky with
Their colorful bands of reds, oranges, blues, and purples.
They are one of the wonders of nature
That everyone can enjoy.
So take a minute and take a look at the clouds.

Sleep

I close my eyes as I try to sleep.
Then I feel the loneliness of the night.
I can't forget that feeling of you close to me.
I need you close to me again.
Let the spirit of love bring you back to me.

Acknowledgments

To all the people who have enjoyed my writings and have encouraged me to compile my book together. Thank you.

About the Author

Charles Asbury and his wife have been married for forty-eight-plus years. They have two daughters, four grandchildren, and four great-grandchildren. He is a veteran of the US Army. Charles has traveled to Europe, Thailand, and Ecuador, South America, and enjoys visiting the Botanical Gardens in Athens with his wife. He enjoys creating pottery at the local community art center pottery studio.

www.ingramcontent.com/pod-product-compliance
Lightning Source LLC
Chambersburg PA
CBHW020535080526
44583CB00013B/868